THE STARS OF LIBERTY

Utah Beach
June 6th 1944

Author of stories, poetry, teenage and adult fiction, winner of several awards, but also a songwriter, **Patrick Bousquet-Schneeweis** splits his time between Hendaye and Paris. His passion for the history of the two world wars is matched only by his passion for cats. Patrick has happily turned his pen to comic books, working alongside Régis Hector to create comics in the *Les aventures d'Oscar et Mauricette* series.

Other titles by Patrick Bousquet-Schneeweis

- *Héros du Jour J*, Orep.
- *La Balle rouge*, préfacé par Raymond Aubrac, Orep.
- *Bleu chien soleil des tranchées*, Serpenoise.
- *Chance, Les ailes de la liberté*, Serpenoise.
- *Les Neiges de l'enfer*, Serpenoise (Prix jeunesse "Raconte-moi l'Histoire" 2008).
- *Un tank nommé Éternité*, Serpenoise.
- *La Banquise a croqué le Chat noir*, Serpenoise (Prix littéraire des Vosges du jeune lecteur 2006).
- *Shootings*, préfacé par Gilles Perrault, Les 3 Orangers (Prix jeunesse "Raconte-moi l'Histoire" 2012).
- *Félin pour l'autre suivi de Même les souris ont du chagrin*, (co-written with his cat Scot) Les 3 Orangers.

Eclectic author, **Michel Giard** has published close to fifty books, the majority of which take maritime history and Normandy as their subject matter. Historian, speaker, globetrotter, reporter for local French radio, Orep Éditions has already published *Phares et feux de Normandie* and *Chansons normandes* by the author.

Other titles by Michel Giard

- *Chansons normandes, du Cotentin à la plaine de Caen*, Orep.
- *Phares et feux de Normandie*, Orep.
- *Les Bateaux du Jour J*, Éditions Sutton.
- *Le Carnet de cuisine du Cotentin*, Le Télégramme.
- *Le Dictionnaire du Cotentin*, Le Télégramme.
- *Les Mousses, de Colbert à nos jours*, Le Télégramme.
- *Prendre pied, tenir ou mourir*, Éditions P. Galodé.
- *Les Grandes Catastrophes maritimes du XXe siècle*, Éditions P. Galodé.
- *La Carriole*, Éditions Isoète.

Patrick Bousquet-Schneeweis & Michel Giard

THE STARS OF LIBERTY

Utah Beach
June 6th 1944

OREP
EDITIONS

Zone tertiaire de Nonant - 14400 BAYEUX
Tel: 02 31 51 81 31 - **Fax:** 02 31 51 81 32
info@orepeditions.com - www.orepeditions.com

Editor: Grégory PIQUE
Conception design: Éditions OREP
Graphics and layout: Sophie YOUF
Editorial coordination: Cécile VIVANT
English translation: Claire SCAMMELL / Mélanie CHANAT

*"... The war will be won or lost on these beaches...
We have only one chance to defeat the enemy
and it's when they are in the water..."*
                              Field Marshal Rommel.

Foreword

This text, which has been carefully researched, is a work of fiction.

The authors

Acknowledgements

Thank you to Benoît Noël from the Utah Beach D-Day museum for his insightful comments during the editing of this book.

*For Mum, Scot and Twiny, whose absence
is felt, and for Anne and Mélanie,
whose presence is cherished.*

P. B-S.

*To my son Guillaume, that he may always
remember the beaches of Normandy.*

M.G.

The alert

27th of April 1944

Night has fallen over Cherbourg, plunged into darkness by orders of the German occupier. Even the lights which once marked out the channels of the largest artificial harbour in the world have been extinguished.

It is 10pm.

Six fast torpedo boats of the 5th flotilla and three of the 9th flotilla, the famous *Schnellboots*, leave the harbour through the west exit after visiting the arsenal.

Their crews were put on alert at 7:30pm when a *Luftwaffe*[1] reconnaissance aircraft detected an enemy convoy off the coast of Devon, to the east of Plymouth.

The information was immediately transmitted to the *Kriegsmarine*[2] in Cherbourg, then to the *Kapitänleutnant*[3] Wilhelm Boese, commander of this flotilla of fast torpedo boats, the terror of the Allied fleet.

---

1. German air force.
2. German navy.
3. Captain of the Germany navy.

Kapitänleutnant Rudolf Petersen had made sure that the 21 crew members were at their posts on board each of the boats.
The engines are running under the attentive and experienced eye of the mechanics.
Preparations had been carried out far from prying eyes in a concrete shelter which previously housed French submarines. A strong current of air swept through the shelter and a sinister humidity dripped from the walls and stuck to the Germans' clothes.

A few minutes later, this unpleasant feeling is being blown away by the sea air.
On board the S-boots there is no small talk.
Every marine is well trained, hardened, aware of his responsibilities.
If the soldiers allow their minds to wander, for the younger men it is to a fiancée left behind in Germany, or, for the lucky ones, to a French girlfriend.
Bootsmaat[4] Gunther Zimmerman is one of the lucky ones.
He met Viviane, a young hairdresser, in the Café du Théâtre eight months ago; they have been inseparable ever since.
When the couple walk down Rue Albert Mahieu together it is to a stream of jibes.

---

4. Petty officer in the German navy.

This young Frenchwoman in a flimsy dress dating a German marine, the shame!
Sometimes when he hears these mocking comments Gunther will turn around and look the culprit right in the eyes, who more often than not then quickly turns their gaze to the ground.
What can they say? What can they do? Nothing, except bear it! To revolt would be suicide, every Frenchman knows it.
To criticise openly is forbidden. *Verboten!*

*

The waves crash violently and rhythmically into the hull of the S100 fast torpedo boat as it opens the course for the boats behind.
To the boats' port sides are the Landemer cliffs. But where are they headed? Towards the islands of Jersey or Guernsey which have been occupied since July 1940? Has there been a commando raid against one of the islands or a mutiny at the labour camp on Alderney?
So many questions race through young Gunther's mind.
In any case, they were preparing for something out of the ordinary. That much was certain.

Instead of pushing west into the Race of Alderney, the S-boots speed northwards, their engines at full throttle.

In his tiny cabin next to the charthouse, each radio operator keeps contact with base.

"This is S-boot 100..."
"This is S-boot 143..."
"This is S-boot 140..."

Around midnight, the German boats approach their target and launch several rockets in the direction of the Allied convoy.

Then, night gradually descends over the Channel.

Operation *Tiger*

The failure of the Canadian raid on Dieppe on the 19th of August 1942 had taught the Allies the difficulty of seizing a port under enemy fire; Prime Minister Churchill had deplored the slaughter.
The coming landings must be carried out on a larger front, with better trained troops.
For this next attempt, which would take place in 1944, a full rehearsal was vital.
Eisenhower, on the American side, and Montgomery,[5] on the British, were in agreement. There was no question about it.
It is April 1944, operations *Duck* and *Beaver* have been completed; the third operation, code named *Tiger*, is about to commence.

The first wave of this new operation involves the paras of the 101st and the 82nd Airborne Divisions jumping out over the English countryside close to the sea, with the objective of opposing the maritime forces who will be deployed to confront them.

---
5. See Key figures, pages 68-69.

Their opponents will be soldiers of the 4th American Infantry Division accompanied by an engineer brigade.

During the afternoon of the 27th of April, the GIs[6] take their place on board the eight LSTs[7] which make up convoy T4, which, unfortunately, has been detected by the German air force.
Boarding is completed at Torbay, between Brixham and Torquay, before the convoy sets out to sea, leaving Plymouth and Eddystone lighthouse behind it.
In Devon, the entire area bordering Slapton Sands where operation *Tiger* will be carried out is classified top secret.
The area is closed to civilians. The villages have been evacuated and the roads closed.

"Rehearsal!" announced a young, athletic captain to his men.
Leonard T. Schroeder, just 25 years old, was born in Maryland on the 16th of July 1918. The 4th infantry division was like a second family to him.
He had joined the unit as a second lieutenant but was soon promoted.
"Men", he said to them, "this is the third

---
6. American soldiers.
7. See glossary, page 72.

exercise we are carrying out in order to prepare for the final assault, the opening of a second front to the west.
"And what happens then?" asked Private Ron Northwood naively, a freckle-faced kid just 20 years of age.
"You'll see!"
Schroeder resumed his address to F Company of the 2nd Battalion of the 8th Infantry Regiment:
"During operation *Tiger*, the conditions will be exactly as they will be during the actual landing and the exercise will be carried out using real bullets. So watch your backs! Got that, Ron?"

Night has fallen over the counties of Dorset and Devon.
The soldiers gaze up at the starry sky while Schroeder passes slowly from group to group.
"Go and get some rest! Tomorrow you'll be up at 5am ready to carry out operation *Tiger* on a long sandy beach which looks a lot like another beach you'll set foot on very soon."

*

28th of April, 1:30am
The HMS *Scimitar* destroyer accompanying convoy T4 reports structural damage requiring a return to base.

"Roger that. You have permission to return. Anything to report?"
"A few rockets around an hour ago. Apart from that, everything is OK."
HMS *Scimitar* turns around, leaving T4 convoy under the escort of HMS *Azalea*.

1:45am
On the Portsmouth radar screens watchmen have detected fast torpedo boats approaching Lyme bay, between Torbay and Portland.
Almost immediately an anxious voice is heard over the airwaves:
"This is LST 515, reporting tracer bullet fire towards the rear of the convoy".
"Roger that".
"This is LST 507, reporting tracer bullet fire".
"Don't worry, folks. I think the fire must be part of the night exercise, no doubt to make sure you stay vigilant."
As these words were spoken, on board S-boots 136 and 140 the marines were busy preparing the first torpedoes ready to be fired.

*

2am
"*Feuer!*"
The torpedoes from the two S-boots shoot towards LST 507 which is hit level with the

engine room, to the rear.

It is immediately set ablaze.

"Evacuate ship" ordered a young officer in a blood-stained uniform.

Some of the men launch a few of the rafts, others fasten the belts of their lifejackets and jump into the sea.

Operation *Tiger* is quickly turning into a tragedy.

On board LST 515 and 531, the marines up on the bridge notice the flames devouring the 507.

"Try to contact them", orders the officer of the watch on board LST 531 on his radio. "I would like to know what's going on".

"No response, Lieutenant", came the report a few minutes later. "Perhaps they do not want to communicate, or perhaps their equipment was damaged in the explosion".

"OK, let's continue our route", said the officer, not overly worried. "Is there any coffee left? It could be a long night..."

*

The German marines on S-boots 100 and 143 can now clearly make out the silhouette of LST 531 in the moonlight.

Their movements are precise; launching the

torpedoes has almost become a routine.
"*Feuer!*"
LST 531 is hit in the middle of the hull. As it explodes the torpedo sets the ship, as well as the trucks on board with full tanks of fuel, ablaze.
A frantic race to evacuate the boat and survive in the cold water of the Channel begins.
An absolute nightmare in the middle of the night!
Water floods into the sides of the LST; the boat capsizes and sinks in a matter of minutes.

2:20am
Convoy T4 breaks up.
There is no coordination, no centralisation of information. Each LST commander is on his own, unable to locate or identify the attackers. Worse still, in the general panic, LST 496 fires at LST 511 by mistake!
Yet more men are killed and injured needlessly. The fog that descends adds to the general confusion further still.
On board the LSTs every man is now asking himself the same question:
"Could the strike have come from Admiral Donitz's Grey Wolves[8]?"

---

8. Nickname given to the German submarines.

The attack of the S-boots

2:30am
LST 289 fires all its weapons at a German fast torpedo boat that it has finally been able to identify.
But it is too late!
Enemy torpedoes shoot towards the American ship, which is also hit!
The rear of the boat is destroyed; the 40mm gun platform is smashed to pieces. The metal superstructure shatters like glass.
"Launch the LCVPs[9]!" orders an officer from the bridge. "And do it quick, for goodness sake!"
One after the other, five landing craft are launched into the sea and positioned next to the LST. Cargo nets are installed along the hull.
In small groups, the soldiers climb down into the landing craft.
Then LST 289 leaves the convoy in an attempt to return to Dartmouth and tend to its wounds.

---
9. See glossary, page 72.

02:37am
The German fast torpedo boats now decide to attack LST 58 which holds Captain Schroeder and his men.
The ship's commander, having detected the enemy threat, orders:
"Reverse the engines! Hard a starboard!"
"That was close", he adds, seeing a torpedo pass just in front of the bow.
Soon afterwards, Schroeder hears the rumble of the torpedo boats' powerful diesel engines moving away.
He climbs up to the bridge.
"What's happening, commander?"
"The convoy has been attacked by S-boots or submarines. The boat is damaged. At least two other boats have sunk."
"Our escort ships haven't responded?"
"I don't believe so, Captain. For the moment there is no question of launching the landing craft. As to the remainder of the exercise, we will await orders."

3:00am
The German torpedo boats leave Lyme bay and head back to Cherbourg.
For the men on board it is the end of a very successful operation.
Half an hour later, as best as it can, convoy T4 reforms.

On board HMS *Azalea*, a corvette escort vessel, Lieutenant George Geddes asks the authorities for help rescuing the hundreds of shipwrecked sailors struggling to stay alive in the freezing water.
Almost at the very same moment, on their return to Cherbourg, the S-boots are attacked by rockets from a *Beaufighter* bomber.
One of the rockets hits its target. An S-boot explodes.
B*ootsmaat* Gunther Zimmerman will never again see Cherbourg or his girlfriend's pretty little face with those bewitching blue eyes.
Later on the same *Beaufighter* will sink a second S-boot, killing 21 German marines.

4:40am
LST 515 returns to the site of the tragedy accompanied by the British destroyer HMS *Onslow*.
A quarter of an hour later, HMS *Azalea* joins them.
Sadly, there are few survivors for the boats to collect.

Dawn finally breaks over Slapton Sands.
Operation *Tiger* can continue.
A group of young soldiers are gathered around Captain Schroeder, including Ramon Ortega from New Mexico, Frank Douedytis from

Pennsylvania and Ron Northwood from Arkansas.

On the beach tanks are being unloaded by the dozen from LCTs while Jeeps and infantrymen are unloaded from the LCVPs.

Behind them, like an army of ghosts, only the looming shapes of the sunken LSTs bear witness to the drama of the night before.

Overlord[10]

Arriving at the dunes bordering the vast beach at Slapton Sands, Leonard T. Schroeder bore a grim expression.
"The exercise turned into a catastrophe! What on earth is going on?" He asks Colonel MacNeely. "Last night the *Fritz*[11] were shooting at us like rabbits!"
"I know. There was only one ship to escort us. 8,000 men at sea and no means to respond to the enemy attack. And then there was the fog! Everything, unfortunately, conspired against us".
"We must have suffered major losses. And those poor souls who jumped into the water; I fear hypothermia took as many lives as the explosions."
"Captain Schroeder, you are most certainly right. But for now, the order is simple. Radio silence whilst we await orders, whether from the divisional or the Combined Operations headquarters. OK? I am counting on you to do what is necessary."

---
10. See glossary, page 73.
11. Pejorative name for the Germans.

Schroeder wasn't aware of it at that time, but the tragedy had been the result of British and American radios operating on different frequencies, communication difficulties between the navy and the army and insufficient resources sent to rescue the shipwrecked men.

However, and despite the terrible losses – 749 men were killed, two LSTs were sank and a brigade of amphibious tanks was destroyed – the disaster of operation *Tiger* was not only quickly forgotten, but for a long time not spoken of at all by the very highest authorities.

*

On the 8th of May 1944, in front of the entire staff of the Allied headquarters, Eisenhower announced that operation *Overlord* was scheduled for Sunday the 5th of June with the possibility of just two days delay.
This window offered the best conditions possible – a full moon night for the airborne troops, a dawn attack at low tide and a low tidal range[12].

The next day, the head of the 8th US Infantry Regiment, Colonel James Van Fleet, explained

---

12. The difference in sea level between low and high tide.

to his officers that preparations for the landings must be accelerated at all cost.

His orderly distributed army photographs of the coast so that the men could see the zone they would be attacking.

"Gentlemen, I must share some information with you", Van Fleet began. "When General Montgomery arrived in London on the 3rd of January he learnt that the invasion plan was based on a limited assault in three sectors for a front of modest dimensions. He campaigned for an attack with five assault forces for a front that is twice as long. All this has required lots of adjustments and compromises as you can imagine. We will therefore land in one of the two new sectors, the one that is furthest west. Its code name is Utah. Of course this information is top-secret."

The men's expressions were grave. To hide their nerves and apprehension, some of them played with their Zippo lighter, others stared at their shoes. Van Fleet let his officers digest what he had told them before continuing:

"On the naval side, Allied Forces will be placed under the authority of Admiral Ramsay[13]. The US Navy will, of course, play a role, but the bulk of the operation lies with the Royal Navy, with the help of our allies in Europe and

---

13. See Key figures, page 69.

Canada. One last thing... As a result of this new programme being adopted, the opening of a second front[14] to the west has been delayed for one month. I wish you a pleasant afternoon Gentlemen and thank you for your attention."

At this time, alert to Nazi spies, the Allies were practicing disinformation. On the 29th of April, Churchill summoned to 10 Downing Street[15] the men responsible for operation *Fortitude*, a huge bluff which led the Germans to believe the landings would take place in Pas-de-Calais rather than Normandy.
Hundreds of rubber tanks, wooden guns, fake planes, docks and boats appeared as if by magic in various locations across the south of England.
And, in case the deception was not convincing enough, men who doubled for generals, such as Meyrick Clifton James, who could easily pass for Montgomery, sometimes went to inspect them.

*

During the daily briefings held in the lead up to the landings, the GIs familiarised themselves

---
14. Van Fleet is referring to the landings in Provence which would finally take place on the 15th of August 1944.
15. The official residence of the British prime minister.

with the countryside and sectors where they would be fighting.

"It's crazy how much this beach looks like Slapton Sands where we landed during operation *Tiger*", commented young Ron Northwood, looking at an army map.
"You're not wrong, son," said Captain Schroeder. "We just have to hope that the approach will be less deadly than we experienced a few weeks ago!"

Moose and Teddy

1st of June 1944

Every evening, on BBC radio, aired the programme *Les Français parlent aux Français* (*the French talk to the French*).

The programme transmitted cryptic messages, "*The Michelin map is becoming more and more rare*"[16], some were cheerful, "*We're going to Paris to see the fireworks*"[17] and others melancholy, "*The long sobs of Autumn's violins...*"[18]

Through these short messages, the French Resistance[19] was quickly mobilised; instructions were issued and weapons and explosives were snuck out of their hiding places.

German spies kept a close ear to the broadcasts and were successful in decrypting a number of the messages.

Thus, when the verse "*The long sobs of Autumn's violins...*" was read out on air, the 15th army,

---

16. *La carte Michelin devient de plus en plus rare.*

17. *Nous irons à Paris voir le feu d'artifice.*

18. *Les sanglots longs des violons de l'automne.*

19. The network of underground movements formed in France during the Second World War to fight against the German occupying forces and collaborationist Vichy government.

which controlled the coastline from the mouth of the Escaut to the mouth of the Dives, was put on alert.

Then the information was relayed to Hitler's GHQ and von Rundstedt's[20] headquarters, commander of the 60 divisions positioned to the west. However, von Rundstedt, having received countless pieces of false information since the start of the year, didn't take any action. In fact, he continued to dismiss the information, to the point of, on the morning of the 5th of June, saying to one of his deputies: "With this bad weather over the Channel, there is nothing to suggest an invasion is imminent". Meanwhile...

*

Captain Schroeder was feeling dejected.

He was suffering from a nasty fever and the medic attached to his company had just made a decision he was extremely unhappy about.

"Captain, you cannot stay here in this condition. I am going to send you to the depot; the medics there will have you back on your feet in a few days."

"The depot? Do you know what that means?" protested Schroeder. "The men who go

---

20. See Key figures, page 70.

there don't return to their units once they've recovered, they are put on reserve! Do what you have to do, but I am not going to miss D-Day!"

"Captain, I understand you are angry and disappointed, but there are times in life when you have to be reasonable."

Like death warmed up and cursing all the while, Schroeder eventually followed the medic.

At the end of the day, sent by his fellow soldiers, Private Ron Northwood went to see how Schroeder was feeling.

"Hey, kid..." said Schroeder quietly as Ron was leaving "...call General Theodore Roosevelt[21]. Explain my situation. Tell him if there is anything he can do I would be eternally grateful..."

2nd June 1944

At daybreak, the boarding of troops began at every port in southern England.

The 8th Regiment of the 4th US Division headed for Torbay without delay.

After hours of waiting and having their packs and weapons checked, the men of the 2nd Battalion finally boarded the *USS Barnett*.

---

21. See Key figures, page 70.

The next day, a Jeep carrying Teddy Roosevelt stopped in front of the 8th Regiment infirmary.
"Is Captain Schroeder here?"
"Yes, General. Second tent, bed 19. You can't miss him."
Suffering from acute arthritis, Theodore Roosevelt Jr, son of the former US president and cousin to the current president, Franklin Delano Roosevelt[22], walked with difficulty with the help of a cane.
Arriving at Schroeder's bed, he said with a wink:
"Moose[23], my boy, get yourself dressed and get moving! My Jeep is outside".
The two men left the tent under the eyes of disinterested sentries.
'Moose' Schroeder resumed his place within the battalion immediately. He received a dossier containing photos of the landing zone in Utah sector and the routes to take as a priority when leaving the beach.
At this time Teddy Roosevelt was also attempting to convince Raymond O. Barton, head of the 4th ID, to let him participate in *Overlord*.
Having run out of arguments, Roosevelt finally took a new tack:

---

22 See Key figures, page 70.

23. Captain Schroeder was nicknamed 'Moose', after an animal known for its strength.

"Ray, I'm begging you, I have to go! Believe me, it will reassure the troops to have me there. They have gotten used to me being there during training, I can't abandon them now!"

"OK, OK, Teddy, don't get worked up! You have my green light, you old devil!" conceded Barton, putting his hand on Roosevelt's shoulder. "Good luck to you and your men!"

However, at dawn on the 4th of June, Eisenhower decided, much to his regret, to delay the landings on account of the appalling weather conditions.

Let's go!

In woods near Southwick House, Eisenhower, exhausted, finally fell to sleep in his trailer. He had spent all day talking to meteorological specialists in the hope that the weather would soon improve.

On the 5th of June, at 3 o'clock in the morning, he woke up having barely slept, put on his battledress and, in driving rain, jumped into his Jeep and headed to the headquarters. He entered the library accompanied by three meteorologists, including Group Captain James Stagg of the Royal Air Force.

"Gentleman", announced Stagg, "the situation is evolving very quickly. A new front from the Atlantic is moving towards the Channel. There will be a slight improvement tomorrow in air and sea conditions. In short, we will have a period of over 24 hours where the weather is a bit more favourable, or, let's say, less unfavourable".

For barely a quarter of an hour the general officers debated the arguments for and against, the likely, the possible and the improbable.

Finally, Eisenhower, full of emotion and conscious of the enormous responsibility on his shoulders, addressed the room:
"Gentlemen, I am deeply persuaded that we must give the order to begin the operation. It seems to me that we don't have a choice. OK, let's go!"
The meeting over, Ike returned to his trailer, racked with emotion. The coming day might just be the most important day of his life...

*

The minute the order was given, the Allied operation was underway.
On board the *USS Barnett*, as on all the other ships, the phone rang.
"This time, men, it's the call we've been waiting for!" announced a sergeant to the group of infantrymen around him.
The men immediately began clapping and cheering.
The ship took its place in the huge armada headed for Piccadilly Circus,[24] where the convoys would be assembled before following the channels cleared and marked out by minesweepers.

---

24. See glossary, page 73.

5th of June, 6pm
Captain Schroeder could not believe his eyes. The sea was completely covered with ships! It was an extraordinary sight!
As a *Typhoon* squadron thundered overhead, Schroeder turned to his neighbour and said: "Just imagine, I could have missed this!"

At that moment, the first paras of the 101st Airborne Division were lining up alongside the C-47s[25] at the airbase in Slapton Sands.
Slapton Sands was a place that held dark memories for those who, like Schroeder, experienced the drama of operation *Tiger* first-hand.
The *Screaming Eagles*[26] moved in single file toward the aircraft which would take them over Sainte-Marie du Mont, close to the villages of Saint-Martin-de-Varreville, Hiesville and Angoville-au-Plain.

Their mission was to occupy the zone behind Utah Beach and to control the routes leading inland from the sea.
With a bit of luck, they would quickly effect the junction with the soldiers who would be landing at Utah the next morning.

---

25. See glossary, page 72.
26. Nickname of the paratroopers in the 101st Airborne Division.

On the 5th of June, at 9:15pm, the BBC aired its daily programme.
These were the messages; "*It is hot in Suez*"[27], "*The tomatoes need to be picked*"[28], "*The dice are down*"[29], and finally, the message everyone was so anxious to hear, the second verse of Verlaine's poem:
"*Wound my heart with a monotonous languor...*"[30]
I repeat: "*Wound my heart...*"

The German 15th army's radio-listening service picked up this message but, once again, did not react.
Anyway, who would have been crazy enough to believe that the Allies would have attempted the landing in such dreadful weather, and announce the invasion on BBC radio?!
The day before, Rommel had returned to Germany to celebrate his wife's birthday!
Who could have imagined that at that moment in England, C-47s and Horsas[31] packed full of paratroopers – 13,000 Americans and 5,300 British – were taking off at great pace.
Who could have believed that a formidable armada of 6,300 boats was crossing the Channel?

---

27. Il fait chaud à Suez.
28. Les tomates doivent être cueillies.
29. Les dés sont sur le tapis.
30. Blessent mon cœur d'une langueur monotone.
31. See glossary, page 72.

Who would have thought that thousands of men were converging towards Normandy where they would meet their destiny?

A very quiet beach

5th June 1944, 7:15pm
On the beach at Sainte-Marie-du-Mont, in the WN5 bunker occupied by a section of the 3rd Company of the 919th Germany Infantry Regiment, it was dinner time.
Quietly anxious and without an appetite, Lieutenant Arthur Jahnke was eating dinner with his men.
Later that night, he couldn't sleep with the noise of the hundreds of planes flying constantly overhead.
Janhke tried to reassure himself by thinking about the weapons the WN5 bunker had at its disposal, an 88mm tank gun, anti-tank rifles and submachine guns, not to mention the formidable *Goliaths*[32] that he had recently received.
His gloomy thoughts were suddenly interrupted by the phone ringing.
"I have been alerted to the presence of enemy paras in your sector", announced an

---

32. Small remote-controlled vehicles packed with explosives.

Oberleutnant[33] based in Saint-Lô with a rasping voice.

"What do you mean, paras? Can't you give me any more information?"

"Unfortunately not. But the information seems reliable. Can you verify the sighting?"

"OK, I'll take care of it", replied Jahnke. "I will dispatch a patrol and keep you updated."

An hour later, the patrol returned having captured twenty or so *Screaming Eagles* who had been dropped off a bit too early and in the middle of nowhere by a pilot terrified by *Flak*[34] fire.

But it was impossible for Jahnke to relay the information back to Saint-Lô. The telephone line had been cut, no doubt by the Resistance. From here on in, Jahnke and his men were on their own.

*

At midnight on the 6th of June, 1,200 bombers attacked the coastal batteries and fortifications in the Utah Beach sector.

At one o'clock in the morning, the crews of Squadron 342 Lorraine attended a final briefing.

---
33. This rank corresponds to that of a sub-lieutenant.
34. German anti-aircraft defence.

"Gentlemen", began an RAF officer wearing a highly decorated uniform. "Your mission is to lay a covering smoke screen between the invasion fleet and the German defences, from the headland at Barfleur to the Saint-Marcouf islands, in order to protect the beach known under code name Utah. Remember, the Channel will be covered with boats. Take flares to identify your position in case you need them.
Take off at 5:10am. Good luck everyone!"

Prelude to the assault

'Moose' Schroeder had just finished writing a letter to his wife Margaret, he asked her to take care of his 18-month-old son in case anything should happen to him. He looked up from his letter and around at his men.
He was struck by the calm that the men exuded, men who would in just a few hours' time be looking death in the eye.
Some of them were playing cards, others daydreaming or talking quietly to their neighbours. Others were gathered around the chaplain seeking spiritual guidance or writing to their loved ones.
There were others too sharpening their bayonets or checking the mechanisms and cartridge clips on their weapons.

At 3:30am, a wave of bombers attacked the WN5 strongpoint. The bombs hit weapon stores, one of the anti-tank rifles and the 88 mm gun.
"Everything is *kaput*, Lieutenant" reported an experienced soldier who had fought in the war

on the Eastern Front, once the veil of sand and dust had finally settled.

A few minutes later, enormous naval canons targeted the WN5 strongpoint, causing more death and destruction.

But the worst was yet to come...

At 4am, the inhabitants of La Madeleine, a village next to the beach, terrorised by the violence of the continuous bombings, took shelter in a farm next to the mayor's house.

On the south coast of England, Captain Schroeder's men were boarding the *USS Barnett*.

Whilst he was overseeing the boarding of his soldiers, Schroeder saw his friend General Teddy Roosevelt approach him discreetly.

"Moose, take me on board your boat", Teddy implored him. "I am sure if you look hard enough you can find room for me".

"OK, General. In a few minutes you can get on".

"Listen, my friend..." said Roosevelt shortly afterwards to the landing craft's pilot, "...try to take us to land without too much damage. Above all, avoid those damned mines planted on the obstacles. We didn't come this far to end up in a heap of twisted metal and flames!"

5:13am

The crews of Squadron Lorraine could make out the grey waters of the Channel beneath their aircraft.

With the sea beneath them and the canopy of shells above, the planes were flying in the direction of the streaks of searchlights lighting up the coast.

They left behind them a thick screen of smoke which obscured an area of around ten kilometres of the Utah Beach zone.

5:58am

As dawn breaks over the Channel, the sky is grey, the wind cold and the sea white with foam.

For the German soldiers, the respite was brief. Following the shelling from the 9th US Air Force in their 275 B26 Marauders, the battleship *Nevada* and the destroyers accompanying it opened fire simultaneously on the coastal defences.

In front of them, the men of the 4th ID were just beginning to make out the dim line of Utah Beach.

The assault

6:28am
Captain Schroeder's landing craft scraped the sand and came to a sudden stop, stuck on a sandbank.
Without panicking, in spite of the gunfire and explosions all around them, the pilot asked the soldiers to leave the LCVP urgently.
Schroeder was the first off.
In waist-deep water and around ten metres in front of his men, holding his Colt 45, Schroeder moved through the hail of gunfire, as quickly as possible, towards the shore.
It was an historic moment; two minutes before zero hour, without knowing it, Schroeder was the first American soldier to set foot on the Normandy front.
At the same time, from his shell-destroyed trench, Arthur Jahnke watched with alarm as the wall of boats emerged little by little from the fog.
Then, he saw a swarm of landing craft packed with soldiers charging towards him.

The MG 42s[35] hidden in the bunkers just behind the dunes were quickly put into action, ploughing the first bloody furrows among the GIs navigating their way through the obstacles.

Schroeder's men were now advancing without cover.
They had a few hundred metres to cross before finding shelter, or, a few hundred chances of losing their lives...
Young Ron Northwood was one of the first to fall, hit by shrapnel square on the chest, then a sergeant attempting to shelter behind the body of a fellow soldier was taken out by a sniper.
Further along the beach, among the corpses and abandoned weapons and lifejackets, a headless body drifted slowly along the beach.
All around, and as if oblivious to the shower of bullets, medics bravely attempted to go to the aid of the wounded men scattered across the sand.
A few minutes later, 28 amphibious *Sherman* DD tanks[36] arrived on the beach, while the Engineers did their best to clear barbed wire fencing, tetrahedrons[37] and Rommel's

---

35. German sub-machine gun.
36. See glossary, page 73.
37. See glossary, page 73.

asparagus[38] using explosives.
Then the first bulldozers arrived to push back the carcasses of the numerous wrecks which already littered Utah Beach.
Impervious to the surrounding confusion and the infernal noise of explosions, Teddy Roosevelt, a smile on his lips, joined the first men to have arrived on the beach.
Nearby, some enemy soldiers surrendered, panicked by the scale of the bombings, others continued to fight relentlessly.

Around 7am Arthur Jahnke realised that the situation was hopeless.
A few metres away from him, sheltering in an anti-tank ditch, American soldiers invited him to surrender.
Jahnke glanced at the submachine gun lying on the sand in front of him.
One of the GIs, having noticed this, pounced on the German.
"Calm it, *Fritz*! It's over now", he said, tackling him around the waist. "Put your hands above your head and go and sit against the wall over there."
"Move and you're dead!" threatened another GI, gesturing with his Thompson[39].
Captain Schroeder and the battalion's

---
38. See glossary, page 72.
39. American submachine gun.

interpreter had witnessed the scene. Wanting to know more about the enemy weapons deployed in the sector, 'Moose' decided to interrogate Jahnke.

The stubborn lieutenant stared at the horizon silently.

"OK, go to hell!" Schroeder said to him. "I don't have time to waste with…"

He didn't get to finish his sentence, a shell exploded not far from them, sending shrapnel in every direction.

Soon after, on the order of Teddy Roosevelt, who was concerned for their lives, wounded German soldiers were evacuated from the beach, Arthur Jahnke among them.

Before boarding the lifeboat which would take them to a destroyer ship anchored offshore, Jahnke took one last look over Utah Beach and knew that it was all over for Germany.

The injury

At 9am, like at the neighbouring strongpoints WN3 and WN2, German resistance at the WN5 strongpoint had ceased to exist.

A map in his hand, Teddy Roosevelt realised with surprise that the landing craft, which were supposed to have arrived in Saint-Martin-de-Varreville, had in fact landed two kilometres further south, in front of the dunes in La Madeleine.

"It must have been the current", said a moustached colonel, his uniform covered with dust.

"What do you mean, the current?!" replied Roosevelt, steaming with rage. "Now my map is useless! Look, there were supposed to be two roads to take us inland. Here there is only one!"

Without asking any more questions – after all, this navigational error could turn out to be a blessing in disguise – Roosevelt, having decided to make the best of the situation and advance, uttered the famous words:

"We'll start the war from right here!"

*

Gradually as they advanced inland, the GIs came across animals blown to pieces, destroyed farms, lost soldiers, the remains of burnt out vehicles and countless injured enemy soldiers. Suddenly, as he was making his way towards a civilian wearing a beret guiding soldiers across a mine field, Schroeder felt an intense pain shoot across his arm.

He had been hit by two bullets, fired – it seemed – by a soldier waiting in ambush behind a low wall.

The injury was serious and, a few hours later, while unconscious, 'Moose' was evacuated to a field hospital set up next to the beach.

Soon after, he briefly regained consciousness, thought he heard that they were going to have to amputate, and then lost consciousness again.

At the same time in England, the Allied headquarters, through the words of Colonel Dupuy, press officer to General Eisenhower, were preparing to announce the Normandy landings to the world.

*

That morning the paras of the 101st division seized the Saint-Martin de Varreville battery.

Around midday, the first contingent of the 4th ID effected the junction with the paras at Pouppeville bridge.

At around 1pm, the first American tanks entered Sainte-Marie-du-Mont.

When the tanks arrived, the town's children, who had endured years of restrictions and shortages, were met by kind, smiling soldiers handing out all the chocolates, sweets, chewing gum and – not forgetting their parents – cigarettes, they could carry.

"Long live America!" exclaimed a little girl, eagerly holding out her hands to a beaming GI.

*

On the 7th of June 1944, Captain Leonard Schroeder was boarded onto a hospital-ship headed for Falmouth on the south coast of England.

In the days that followed, he underwent five operations. Eventually, the surgeons managed to save his arm.

"Doctor", began Leonard during his daily check-up, "I want to go back to be with my men. We slept, ate and breathed together for three years before landing in Normandy…"

"Now, Captain…"

"How can I explain it to you? I lost a lot of

my men on Utah Beach. We were united back then, sometimes closer than members of a family... Today these same soldiers are still fighting in Normandy and no doubt waiting for me to return. Can you make sure that..."
"Absolutely not, Captain!" replied the doctor. "It is still too early. Your injury is far from healed. You need to have a bit of patience, for goodness' sake!"
"But..."
"No buts! One day, perhaps, you'll thank me".

An American hero

A few days after the 6th of June, when the Allied bridgehead had been well established, the Pentagon decided to find out the identity of the first GI to have invaded Western Europe. It was decided that it was Leonard T. Schroeder Jr. Immediately, American journalists started to rummage around his past as a student and early military career.
They quickly discovered that Schroeder was married.
It wasn't long before the phone rang at 906 Carolina Avenue in North Augusta, a small town in South Carolina.
Everyone wanted to know more about the woman who shared her life with America's new hero.
Her name was Margaret. A pretty brunette with wavy hair worthy of a movie star. Born in Maryland, she met Leonard at Glen Burnie High School.
Very quickly, the Schroeder family became household names from New York to California.

On the 21st of June, there was a knock at Margaret's door.
A man in a Western Union uniform held out a telegram from the War Department in Washington.
With trembling hands, Mrs Schroeder ripped open the letter and read:
"Regret to inform you your husband captain Leonard T. Schroeder Jr. was on 6 June slightly wounded in action in France. You will be advised as reports of condition are received. Ulio, the Adjutant General..."
Immediately, the young woman, beside herself with worry, broke down in tears.

The following Monday, in a British hospital, a nurse approached Captain Schroeder's bed with a stack of newspapers and magazines sent from the US.
"Captain, you are a hero!" she said admiringly, gesturing with one of the newspapers.
"A hero? Don't talk nonsense, Shirley! The real heroes are dead or fighting on the front!"
"Read it Captain, and you'll see", insisted the nurse.
Schroeder grabbed one of the newspapers and saw he had made the front-page:
Captain Schroeder first to land on French soil from the sea. His wife and son live here!
Reading the article, Leonard felt a wave of

emotion wash over him.
He quickly shook off the feeling and decided he must let Margaret know he was okay.
'Moose' Schroeder asked for an envelope, some paper and a pen and, after thinking for a few moments, decided to speak from his heart and let the letter keep his secret…

Much later...

The military career of 'Moose' Schroeder did not come to a sudden end on a Normandy beach one day in June 1944.
Captain Schroeder went on to fight in the Battle of the Bulge, the invasion of Nazi Germany, the Korean War and then, in the 1960s, the Vietnam War.
In these campaigns he earned the *Silver Star*[40], the *Purple Heart*[41] and the *Medal of Honor*, a medal awarded by the president of the United States.
Fifty years later, in 1994, Schroeder decided to return to the site of the landings.

*

Like Omaha, Juno, Gold and Sword, Utah had become a beach full of memories.
The Normandy Schroeder returned to in 1994

---

40. Medal awarded for gallantry in action against an enemy of the United States.
41. Medal awarded to a soldier wounded in service.

was a peaceful and prosperous region, far removed from the violence and tragedy it had witnessed in that summer of 1944.

That morning, to the cry of seagulls, race horses trotted along the shore marked by memorial stones recalling the sacrifice made by so many young soldiers who crossed the Atlantic to the defence of liberty.

With the help of a cane and in the company of his memories, Schroeder walked along the beach where he had landed under enemy fire. In front of Arthur Jahnke's WN5 bunker, now a museum, 'Moose' came face to face with a Sherman tank, an LCVP landing craft and two tracked amphibious vehicles nicknamed '*Alligators*'[42] underneath flags flapping in the wind.

Later on, overwhelmed by emotion, he saw the faces of his brothers in arms who had lost their lives on Utah Beach or in the Normandy countryside, where every road, every hedge, every house, was a possible hiding place for a mine or a sniper.

The next day, his pilgrimage took Leonard Schroeder to the vast cemetery in Colleville-sur-Mer which overlooks Omaha Beach, where 10,000 American soldiers rest and where the

---

42. See "LVT" in glossary, page 72.

lives of countless other missing soldiers are commemorated.
Slowly, he headed towards a white cross which, in gold letters, bore the name Theodore Roosevelt Jr.
His friend Teddy died in Normandy on the 12th of July 1944 while the Americans were fighting the Battle of the Hedgerows.
Teddy Roosevelt died of a heart attack in the small village of Méautis during a violent counter-attack led by the SS division *Götz Von Berlichingen.*
Captain Schroeder could still hear the voice which had said to him, on the morning of the 6th of June as they were leaving for Utah Beach:
"Moose, take me on board your boat!"

Like so many other veterans, Leonard Schroeder waited until retirement to make this journey.
It was to be his first and only visit to Normandy, as was the promise he made to his wife before boarding the plane to France.
For him, returning to Utah Beach was to reopen a wound he thought had healed, not only the wound of his flesh, but the wound of his sprit, of his heart.
On this day, the 6th of June 1994, speeches and tributes were made by world leaders and

key figures who had travelled from all over the world to commemorate the event.

Schroeder was only there to reflect.

To remember.

To finally make peace with his past as a soldier, a past he would live with until his death in May 2009.

Historical background

Map of the Battle of Normandy

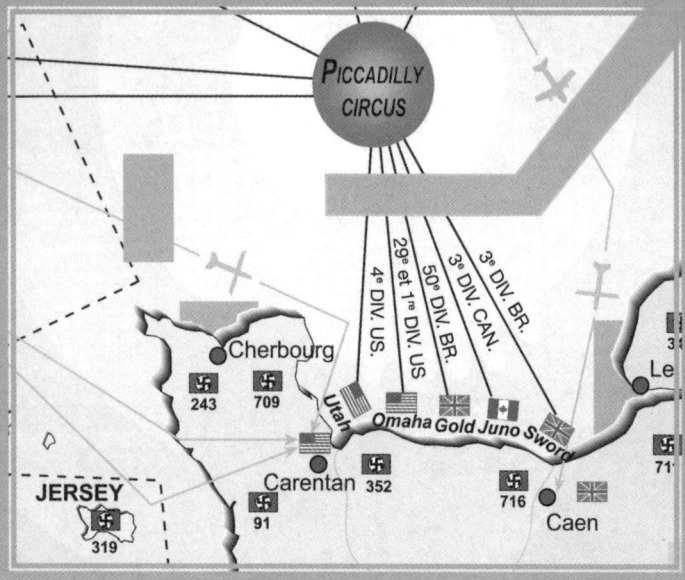

On the 6th of June 1944, at dawn, the Allied invasion fleet appears on the Normandy coast. To the west, American troops of Force "U" land on the beach in La Madeleine in the Utah Beach sector. Force "O" attack the area known as Omaha Beach, which stretches from Vierville-sur-Mer to Sainte-Honorine-des-Pertes. Next along is the British sector, comprising Gold Beach – between Graye-sur-Mer and Arromanches, Juno Beach – between Graye-sur-Mer and Luc-sur-Mer and Sword Beach – between the mouth of the Orne River in Ouistreham and Lion-sur-Mer. It is at Sword Beach that the 177 French soldiers of Commando Kieffer fight the enemy.

Map of Utah Beach sector

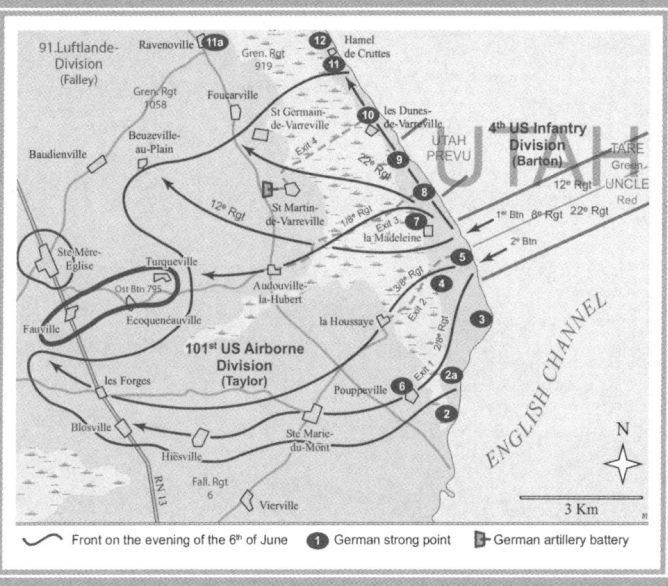

The Utah Beach harbour. The breakwater comprised of old ships ballasted with concrete can clearly be seen in the foreground.

Key figures

Sir Winston CHURCHILL (1874-1965)

British Prime Minister during the Second World War, Churchill announced to his fellow citizens in his inaugural speech on the 13th of May 1940 that he had nothing to offer them but "blood, toil, tears and sweat". He supported General Charles de Gaulle against the Americans. In 1953, he received the Nobel Prize for Literature for his *War Memoirs*.

Dwight D. EISENHOWER (1890-1969)

Known by his officers as "Ike", Dwight Eisenhower was commander of the Allied Forces in Northern Africa and then in Italy. Following the Tehran Conference, he was appointed Supreme Commander of the Allied Forces in Europe and was responsible for preparations for one of the biggest operations in military history: the Normandy landings. After the war he started a very successful career as a politician and was President of the United States from 1952 to 1960.

Charles de GAULLE (1890-1970)

His appeal to the French Resistance on the 18th of June put General de Gaulle in France's history books. Father of Free France, during the war he embodied the image of a France which does not give in to the occupier but continues to fight. Kept out of the final preparations for the landings, he quickly went to Normandy and made an important speech in Bayeux on the 14th of June 1944, in order to pre-empt the intentions of the United States who wanted to put France under their control.

Sir Bernard MONTGOMERY (1887-1976)

It was in the desert sand that Montgomery established his renown thanks to his victory at El Alamein. In January 1944, he was appointed as Eisenhower's deputy, devoting his time and energy to the preparations for the D-Day Landings. He commanded the British troops that were kept at a virtual standstill on the outskirts of Caen for several long weeks.

Bertram RAMSAY (1883-1945)

After leading the Dunkirk evacuation in June 1940, Admiral Ramsay played a major role in preparations for operation *Overlord* and commanded the naval forces during operation *Neptune*.

Erwin Rommel (1891-1944)

After serving in the First World War, Field Marshal Rommel played a key role with the use of tanks in the Battle of France. His presence in Libya, at the head of the *Afrika Korps*, earned him the nickname "Desert Fox". At the end of 1943 he oversaw the German coastal defences, from the Spanish border to the North Sea. He was involved in a plot to assassinate Hitler on the 20th of July 1944 and was later forced to commit suicide.

Franklin Delano ROOSEVELT (1882-1945)

He was elected president of the United States of America for the first time in 1933, then re-elected in 1936 and 1940. He made the decision to take his country to war after the Japanese attack on Pearl Harbor in December 1941. He kept regular contact with Winston Churchill and Joseph Stalin to lead the Allies to their final victory. He died after a long illness a few weeks before Germany surrendered.

Theodore ROOSEVELT Jr. (1887-1944)

General Roosevelt served in the First World War and was wounded at Château-Thierry in the department of Aisne. He then led parallel careers as a businessman and as a politician before re-joining active service in 1941.

He rests in the American cemetery in Colleville-sur-Mer, alongside his brother Quentin, a pilot who was killed in France on the 14th of July 1918.

Gerd von Rundstedt (1875-1953)

Born into a military family, Field Marshal von Rundstedt also chose a career in the armed forces. He served in the First World War and then commanded German troops during the invasion of France in June 1940. After fighting in Russia, he was named commander in chief of the Western front in 1943.

During the Battle of Normandy, von Rundstedt took the nomination of Rommel alongside him, whose views he did not share, badly. Six months later, in December 1944, it was to von Rundstedt that Hitler entrusted the Battle of the Bulge in the Ardennes.

Important dates

January 1933: Adolf Hitler takes power.

September 1939: Start of the Second World War.

May 1940: Invasion of France.

18th of June 1940: General Charles de Gaulle makes his Appeal to the French Resistance.

July to September 1940: Battle of Britain.

7th of December 1941: The US enters the war following the Japanese attack on Pearl Harbor.

8th of November 1942: Allied landings in North Africa.

10th of July 1943: Allied landings in Sicily.

August 1943: Plans for an Allied landing in Normandy are agreed at the Quebec Conference.

6th of June 1944: Allied landings in Normandy.

15th of August 1944: Allied landings in Provence.

22nd of August 1944: End of the Battle of Normandy

25th of August 1944: Liberation of Paris.

December 1944: The Battle of the Bulge.

30th of April 1945: Death of Adolf Hitler in the ruins of Berlin.

8th of May 1945: German surrender.

September 1945: Japan surrenders on the *Missouri* battleship. The Second World War is finally over.

Glossary

Rommel's asparagus: a system of wooden logs, sometimes mined, designed to rip the hull of a landing craft.

C-47 *Dakota*: the Douglas C-47 Skytrain, nicknamed *Dakota*, was used to drop paratroopers on the night of the 5th – 6th of June 1944.

Horsa: british glider. It was *Horsas* that dropped off the soldiers of the 6th Airborne Division near Bénouville Bridge (*Pegasus Bridge*).

Rommel's asparagus

Ike: the nickname of General Eisenhower, Commander-in-Chief of the Allied Forces.

Lancaster: four-engined British bomber; 7,000 were produced between 1941 and 1945. Very effective during night raids.

LCVP: Landing Craft Vehicle & Personnel, the smallest of the landing craft. 11 metres long, it could transport 32 soldiers with their kit.

LST: Landing-Ship Tank, landing ship capable of transporting 2,000 tons of equipment or 6 LCVPs; 98 metres long, the LSTs were equipped with a 40mm gun and several 20mm guns. The double door opening in the bow allowed weapons, vehicles and equipment to be unloaded directly onto the beach.

LVT: Landing Vehicle Tracked *Alligator*. Amphibious landing vehicle mainly used in operations in the Pacific War.

Atlantic Wall: a system of fortifications built by the Germans to prevent and contain the risk of an invasion by sea. During his first inspection, Rommel discovered a number of faults and decided to redesign the main obstacles and defence systems protecting the beaches.

Organisation Todt: established in 1933 by Fritz Todt, the organisation was responsible for all major infrastructure, first in Germany and then in occupied countries. In France, Organisation Todt was heavily involved in building the Atlantic Wall.

Overlord: code name given by the Allies to the landings to the west set as the priority objective during the Quebec conference in 1943.

Piccadilly Circus: on account of its vast numbers, the meeting point for the Allied Armada was named after the famously congested London road junction.

Tetrahedron: concrete obstacle placed on the beaches.

Typhoon: british fighter-bomber. Its rockets made it a formidable "tank-killer".

Schnellboot: known by the Allies as E-boats (or Enemy boats), from 1932 the Schnellboot was the German navy's fast torpedo boat. Equipped with three 4800hp Diesel engines, they could reach a top speed of 48 knots and had a range of 700 nautical miles at a speed of 30 knots. They were used in numerous raids during the Second World War.

Sherman **DD (Duplex Drive):** American tank equipped with 2 rear propellers and a waterproof canvas skirt which meant it was amphibious for up to a few hundred metres.

Main museums about the Battle of Normandy

- **Arromanches:** D-Day museum and 360° circular cinema
- **Bayeux:** Memorial museum of the Battle of Normandy
- **Bénouville:** Café Gondrée
- **Caen:** Peace memorial
- **Catz:** Normandy Tank Museum
- **Cherbourg:** Museum of the Liberation
- **Colleville-sur-Mer:** Overlord Museum
- **Courseulles-sur-Mer:** The Juno Beach centre
- **Douvres-la-Délivrande:** Radar museum
- **Falaise:** Août 44 museum
- **Grandcamp-Maisy:** Rangers museum
- **Merville-Franceville:** Museum of the Battle of Merville
- **Montormel:** Museum of the Battle of Normandy
- **Ouistreham Riva-Bella:** No.4 Commando museum and Museum of the Atlantic Wall, "the Grand Bunker"
- **Quinéville:** Museum of Freedom
- **Ranville:** Pegasus memorial
- **Saint-Côme-du-Mont:** D-Day paratrooper historic centre
- **Saint-Laurent-sur-Mer:** Omaha Beach Memorial museum
- **Sainte-Marie-du-Mont:** Utah Beach D-Day museum
- **Sainte-Mère-Église:** Airborne museum
- **Ver-sur-Mer:** America Gold Beach museum
- **Vierville-sur-Mer:** Omaha D-Day museum

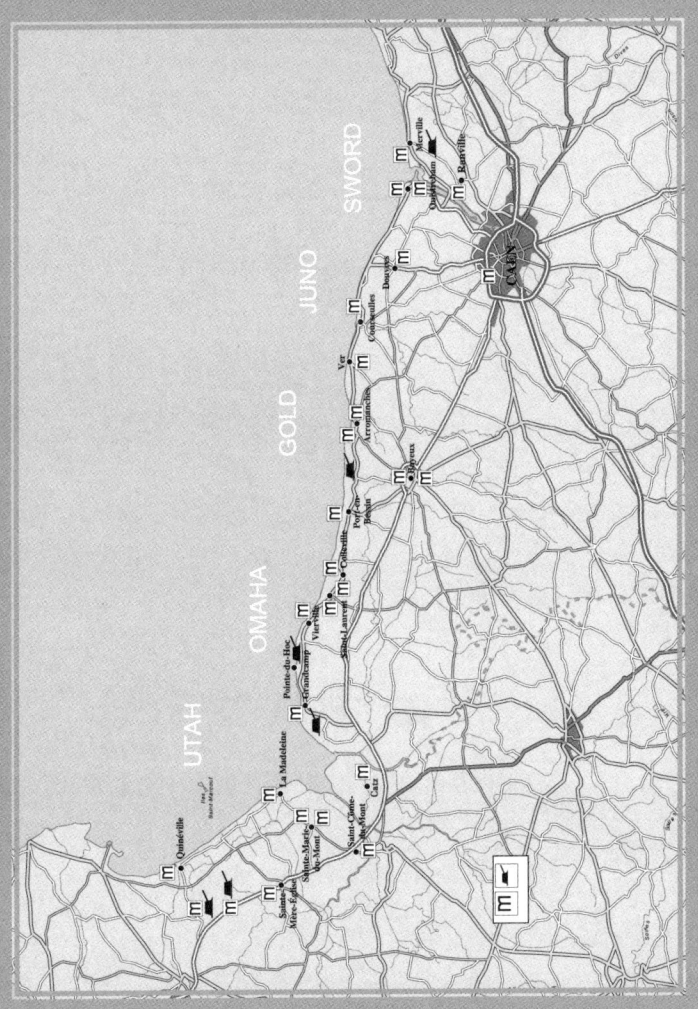

Bibliography

CARELL Paul, *Ils arrivent*, Laffont, 1962.

CAVE BROWN Anthony, *La Guerre secrète, le rempart des mensonges : le Jour J et la fin du IIIe Reich*, Perrin, 2012.

FLORENTIN Eddy, *Le Guide des plages du débarquement et de la bataille de Normandie*, Perrin.

GRANDHOMME Jean-Noël, *Les Malgré-nous de la Kriegsmarine*, La Nuée Bleue, 2011.

HOWARTH David, *6 juin à l'aube*, Presses de la Cité, 1959.

LEMONNIER-GRUHIER François, *La Brèche de Sainte-Marie-du-Mont*, Éditions normandes, 1965.

PERRAULT Gilles, *Le Grand Jour*, J.-C. Lattès, 1994.

PERRAULT Gilles, *Le Secret du Jour J*, Fayard, 1994.

QUELLIEN Jean, *Normandie 44*, Orep, 2011.

QUELLIEN Jean, *Les Américains en Normandie*, Orep, 2012.

RYAN Cornélius, *Le Jour le plus long*, Laffont, 1960.

SHULMAN Milton S., *La Défaite allemande à l'ouest*, Payot, 1948.

Filmography of the Normandy Landings

ESWAY Alexandre, *They are not Angels*, 1947.

FULLER Samuel, *The Big Red One*, 1980.

HANKS Tom, SPIELBERG Steven, *Band of Brothers*, 2001 (10-part mini-series).

MCLAGLEN André Victor, *Breakthrough*, 1978.

PARRISH Robert, *Up from the Beach*, 1965.

SPIELBERG Steven, *Saving Private Ryan*, 1998.

ZANUCK Darryl F., *The Longest Day*, 1962.

Table of contents

The alert 9
Operation *Tiger* 13
The attack of the S-boots 19
Overlord 23
Moose and Teddy 29
Let's go! 35
A very quiet beach 41
Prelude to the assault 45
The assault 49
The injury 53
An American hero 57
Much later... 61

HISTORICAL BACKGROUND

Map of the Battle of Normandy 66
Map of Utah Beach sector 67
Key figures 68
Important dates 71
Glossary 72
Main museums about the Battle
of Normandy 74
Bibliography/Filmography of the
Normandy Landings 76

Dans la même collection

LES ÉRABLES DE SANG
Juno Beach - 6 juin 1944

- Patrick BOUSQUET-SCHNEEWEIS et Michel GIARD
- Format : 130 x 210 mm
- 80 pages intérieures
- Couverture souple
- Dos carré, collé, cousu
- Langues : français, anglais
- Prix : 7,50 €

– Ici Marcel Ouimet de Radio Canada. Je me trouve avec les hommes du régiment de la Chaudière devant une petite station balnéaire nommée Bernières-sur-Mer. Des tirs d'obus en provenance des batteries allemandes s'intensifient autour de nous ! L'ordre de l'assaut est enfin donné ! J'imagine l'émotion de nos valeureux soldats en ces instants historiques car, pour beaucoup, dans leurs veines, coule du sang français…
De Montréal à Juno Beach, l'incroyable odyssée des Canadiens qui, le 6 juin 1944, nous ont aidés à recouvrer notre liberté…

UNE PLAGE EN ENFER
Omaha Beach - 6 juin 1944

- Patrick BOUSQUET-SCHNEEWEIS et Michel GIARD
- Format : 130 x 210 mm
- 80 pages intérieures
- Couverture souple
- Dos carré, collé, cousu
- Langues : français, anglais
- Prix : 7,50 €

Je m'appelle William Bishop. J'appartiens à la 1re division d'infanterue américaine, la fameuse « Big Red One ». Nous sommes le 6 juin 1944 et, dans quelques minutes, je vais débarquer sur la plage d'Omaha la sanglante… Voici mon histoire…

GO ! GERONIMO !
Sainte-Mère-Église - 6 juin 1944

- Patrick BOUSQUET-SCHNEEWEIS et Michel GIARD
- Format : 130 x 210 mm
- 80 pages intérieures
- Couverture souple
- Dos carré, collé, cousu
- Langues : français, anglais
- Prix : 7,50 €

« Steve, qui devait être le premier à franchir la porte du C-47, sentit son cœur battre la chamade. Cette fois, il n'était plus question de reculer.
– Go !, fit le largueur en lui tapant sur l'épaule.
– Geronimo !, s'écria Barrow en plongeant dans le vide obscur de la nuit.
Très vite, le ciel de Normandie se constella de centaines de corolles… »

Revivez la formidable épopée des paras de la 82e aéroportée qui sautèrent sur Sainte-Mère-Église dans la nuit du 5 au 6 juin 1944…

LES DIABLES DE PEGASUS
Pont de Bénouville - 6 juin 1944

- Patrick BOUSQUET-SCHNEEWEIS et Michel GIARD
- Format : 130 x 210 mm
- 72 pages intérieures
- Couverture souple
- Dos carré, collé, cousu
- Langues : français, anglais
- Prix : 7,50 €

Dans le planeur n° 1, les soldats se tenaient par le bras dans l'attente du formidable choc que ne manquerait pas de se produire lorsque l'avion prendrait contact avec le sol.
Peu après, le Horsa laboura la terre dans une pluie d'étincelles avant de finir sa course à proximité des barbelés qui entouraient le pont.
– Tout le monde dehors ! Grouillez-vous, les gars ! hurla un officier en bondissant de l'appareil…

Partagez l'histoire de la prise du pont de Bénouville avec les hommes de la 6e division aéroportée britannique dans la nuit du 5 au 6 juin 1944.

LES FANTÔMES DE PORT-WINSTON
Arromanches - 6 juin 1944

- Patrick BOUSQUET-SCHNEEWEIS et Michel GIARD
- Format : 130 x 210 mm
- 80 pages intérieures
- Couverture souple
- Dos carré, collé, cousu
- Langues : français, anglais
- Prix : 7,50 €

La vision des vestiges des pontons d'Arromanches embua de larmes les yeux de Julie, qui ne put s'empêcher de frissonner. Les spectres, qu'elle avait pensé exorciser en faisant le voyage jusqu'ici, étaient de retour. Plus présents que jamais…
De la construction du port artificiel d'Arromanches au massacre de la prison de Caen, le matin même du Débarquement, retrouvez les fantômes qui hantent aujourd'hui encore Port-Winston.

Photographic credits

Cover illustrations: Arnaud Gaumet
p.66: Map by CRHQ
p.67: Map by Yann Magdelaine
p.67-70, 72: From Michel Giard's collection
p.75: Map by Orep Éditions

ISBN: 978-2-8151-0197-4

© Éditions OREP 2014

All right reserved - **Legal Deposit:** 2nd quarter 2014

In the same collection

THE BLOODY MAPLES
Juno Beach - June 6th 1944

- Patrick BOUSQUET-SCHNEEWEIS and Michel GIARD
- Format: 130 x 210mm
- 80 inside pages
- Soft cover
- Square back, sewn, pasted
- Language: French, English
- Retail price: €7,50

– 'Marcel Ouimet from Radio Canada here. I am with men from the Régiment de La Chaudière in the small seaside resort of Bernières-sur-Mer. Shellfire from the German artillery batteries is intensifying all around us! The order is finally given to attack!
I can imagine the emotion felt by our troops during these historic moments, for many of them have French blood in them…'

From Montreal to Juno Beach, the incredible Canadian odyssey, which, on the 6th of June 1944, contributed towards our newfound freedom...

THE GHOSTS OF PORT-WINSTON
Arromanches - June 6th 1944

- Patrick BOUSQUET-SCHNEEWEIS and Michel GIARD
- Format: 130 x 210mm
- 80 inside pages
- Soft cover
- Square back, sewn, pasted
- Language: French, English
- Retail price: €7,50

The image of the ruins of Arromanches' artificial port brought tears to Julie's eyes and she began to shudder involuntarily. The ghosts she thought she had exorcised by coming here had returned. And she felt their presence stronger than ever…

From the construction of Arromanches' artificial port to the Caen prison massacre on the morning of D-Day, meet the ghosts which continue to haunt Port Winston today.

THE BEACH TO HELL
Omaha Beach - June 6th 1944

- Patrick BOUSQUET-SCHNEEWEIS and Michel GIARD
- Format: 130 x 210mm
- 80 inside pages
- Soft cover
- Square back, sewn, pasted
- Language: French, English
- Retail price: €7,50

My name is William Bishop. I belong to the US 1st Infantry Division, the famous Big Red One.
Today is the 6th of June 1944 and, in a few minutes, I'll be landing on Omaha Beach, in the Easy Red sector.
A beach that will go down in History as Bloody Omaha...
This is my story…

THE DEVILS OF PEGASUS
Bénouville Bridge - June 6th 1944

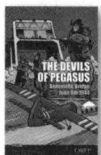

- Patrick BOUSQUET-SCHNEEWEIS and Michel GIARD
- Format: 130 x 210mm
- 72 inside pages
- Soft cover
- Square back, sewn, pasted
- Language: French, English
- Retail price: €7,50

In glider n° 1, the soldiers were braced arm-in-arm ready for the huge impact of the aircraft hitting the ground.
There was a deafening noise as the Horsa ploughed the ground in a shower of sparks before coming to a stop by the barbed wire fence surrounding the bridge.
'Everyone out! Move it lads!' yelled an officer as he leapt out of the glider…
Join the men of the 6th British Airborne Division on their mission to take Bénouville Bridge on the night of the 5th - 6th of June 1944.

GO! GERONIMO!
Sainte-Mère-Église - June 6th 1944

- Patrick BOUSQUET-SCHNEEWEIS and Michel GIARD
- Format: 130 x 210mm
- 80 inside pages
- Soft cover
- Square back, sewn, pasted
- Language: French, English
- Retail price: €7,50

"Steve, who was to be the first to jump through the door of the C-47, could feel his heart beating like a drum. No danger of turning back this time.
"Go!" the dispatcher yelled as he tapped him on the shoulder.
"Geronimo!" cried Barrow as he plunged into the dark of the night.
The Normandy skies were soon to be illuminated by hundreds of garlands…"
Relive the epic feat of the 82nd Airborne paratroopers who jumped out over Sainte-Mère-Église on the night of the 5th to the 6th of June 1944...